THE MUDLARK POEMS & GRAND BUVEUR

Other poetry by Peter Redgrove

The Collector and Other Poems, Routledge, London, 1960.
The Nature of Cold Weather and Other Poems, Routledge, London, 1961.
(*Choice of the Poetry Book Society*)
At the White Monument and Other Poems, Routledge, London, 1963.
The Force and Other Poems, Routledge, London, 1966.
(*Choice of the Poetry Book Society*)
Penguin Modern Poets II. (With D. M. Thomas and D. M. Black) 1968.
Work in Progress, Poet and Printer, London, 1969.
Dr. Faust's Sea-Spiral Spirit and Other Poems, Routledge, London and Boston, 1972.
Three Pieces for Voices, Poet and Printer, London, 1972.
The Hermaphrodite Album (with Penelope Shuttle), Fuller D'Arch Smith, London, 1973.
Sons of My Skin: Selected Poems 1954–74. Edited with an introduction by Marie Peel (Routledge, London and Boston, 1975).
From Every Chink of the Ark: New Poems American and English, (Routledge, London and Boston, 1977).
(*Recommendation of the Poetry Book Society*)
The Weddings at Nether Powers, and Other New Poems, (Routledge, London and Boston, 1979).
(*Choice of the Poetry Book Society*)
The Apple-Broadcast and Other New Poems, (Routledge, London and Boston, 1981).
(*Choice of the Poetry Book Society* and published simultaneously with a recorded cassette)
The Working of Water (Taxus, 1984).
The Man Named East and Other New Poems, (Routledge, London and Boston, 1985).

To Derek Power

THE MUDLARK POEMS & GRAND BUVEUR

from

by

Peter Redgrove

Peter Redgrove

with warmest & best wishes

Feb 87

Rivelin Grapheme Press
London 1986

ACKNOWLEDGEMENTS

Grateful acknowledgements are due to Sylvia Kantaris for help with the French, and to the following books and periodicals, in which some of the poems have already appeared: *Ambit*, *The Manhattan Review*, *New Statesman*, *Poetry International*, *The Politics of Spirit*, *Poly: New Speculative Poetry*, *Spectator*, *Sulfur*, *Temenos*, *The Times Literary Supplement*, *The Working of Water* (*Taxus*).

CONTENTS

page numbers

Chansonnier, ta filleule
C'est ma soif si folle,
Hydre intime sans gueules
Qui mine et désole . . .
J'aime autant, mieux, même,
Pourrir dans l'étang,
Sous l'affreuse crème,
Près des bois flottants.

Rimbaud: '*Comédie de le Soif*'

THE MUDLARK POEMS

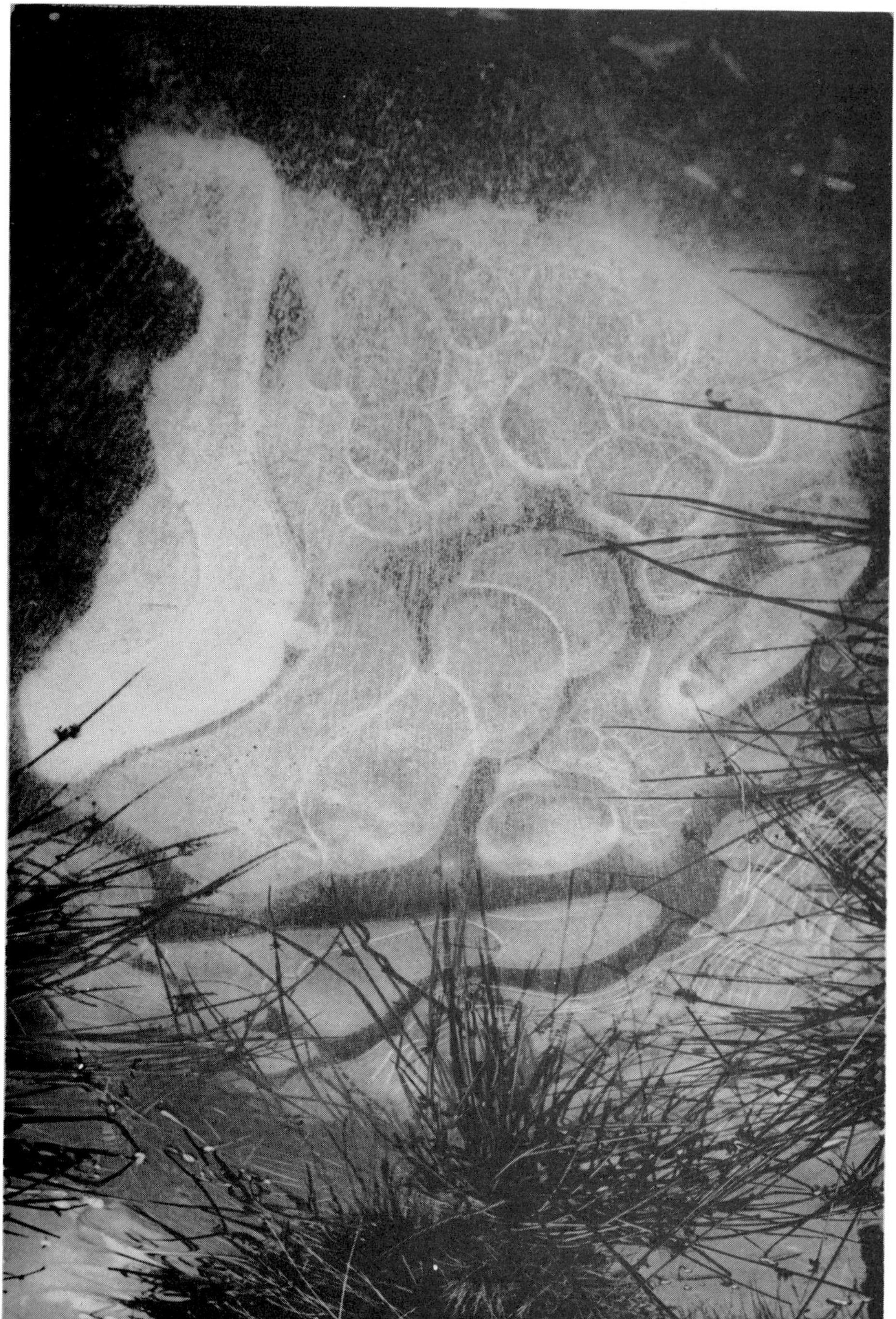

THE FIRST MUDLARK

Swaggering among the distillations,
The resplendent oils of the woodland swamp,
Its water-mirrors and soft turfy bars
That glitter with fire-in-the-dew which is the spirit,

Skipping through
The alcohol swamp by the sea,
With its bubbling glasses,
Dispensary of many many bottles,
All uncorked,
Mixing your medicines with your poisons,

I am body-masked in bacteria and volatilities
And fellow-drinkers, the bacilli are delighted,
They swarm celebrating over Gulliver,
They throw him down again in unction;
It is our fertility-dance, I rise in black.

Who knows how
Rolling in the ploughed field or in the morass
Creates a sexuality which is magic?
Dirt is sexy, and sex not dirty, to this magic;
The fertile slough knows this, and the gleaming fields,
And the ferny bars distil its powers,
Where drunk men plunge through black mirrors
Containing all the possible colours of flowers.

SECOND MUDLARK

I.

I snapped up my watch and made for the door.
White burned from the rock, salt fire,
The sea running like wax,
The white webbing off Trefusis.
The brain cool as dew arranged on a web all night,
Or in the confusion of a brief shower,
The web assembling the scattered water
Parched by a brief sun, regrouping everywhere.
The child, little sage,
Pondering her powdery navel after a bath,
The centre of her web.
The clouds, full of every length of material,
Every pattern, making new vows.
A seagull disappearing against the great shock of apple-blossom,
Reappearing reassembled with a hurtling cry
As white with as many sounds as the clouds are with their
  possibilities,
And the child's cry white with hers,
Regrouping for an instant in her tears,
Regrouping.
In the waterfall's white noise
You hear not only the water
But the ringing shapes of the boulders,
The rattling bed of the stream.
The water rays back on the bow of a bend.
I slide into the mud, black with all possible flowers.

II.

The mud-mirror regroups itself. I wash in the glittering stream. I walk back along the secret woodland path; however, a man of about sixty approaches, strolling his bounding dog. As we near each other, I hail him first, embarassed. The dog-jaws grasp a green bough. I feel a need to explain away my water-rich garments to the dry stroller. 'I fell in the stream', I lie. The spaniel's abundant coat resembles my cloth of brook. 'No, really?' the other remarks indifferently, and passes by. But the dog drops its bough and kisses the back of my woodland-smelling hand with the moist full grip of its lips, the vivid teeth withheld. Then it resumes its swagging bough, and scampers on after its master.

EYE-BESTOWING
(Mudlark III)

Down the small path to the winding marsh
Where the alders bend and lave their heads in mud
He visits for a predawn ritual prayer.
He hoods himself in that same alder-yeast of spring,
Makes of himself a sculptor's rough of mud
With a clod face in which the live eyes beat, rehearsing
The entrance of the sun into the wood, the eye-bestowing;
In the marsh's bubbling spring that feeds
The ferment from a rock, washes off the worst.

For breakfast, bacon
Like sea-sliced strata eaten in the bath.
The child, blood relative
Acting on his behalf in the future, God Willing,
Is learning to read by putting out
Long trains of coloured pictures: witch, jelly, giraffe;
She is also learning vocabulary, it seems,
By touching her Mother.
The ships are drawn up close to the shore;
Great felled trees, are they sleeping, or dead?
The ships are sleeping. The vine
Has smuggled a dew-scroll through the half-open window,
Is shooting arrows made of bees
On a bow made of flowers and bines. In the harbour

Men have busied themselves inside the whales
With their paring-tools; they are drawn up close to the shore
With open mouths and lighted bellies like the naves of churches.
With her, there is the time for playing horse
And the time for stringing pearls. Her blouse
Opens past the pearls into its vaults.
I wash the mud from my head; she says
'You are all eyes.'

THE BIG STORE

I.

The butterflies that feed on sheep-dung,
Oily sheep-dung, and spread more gorgeous rainbows
Across their backs, more plangent velvets;
There are the flints cracked into blue and white
Like sky underground, butterfly-wing blue;
There is the flint-mine full of sealed firmaments,
And the blue thistle bursting out of the sealed mine,
In its choking collar like a fountain of sky;
And there are the bright butterflies that live on oil
Of lighted ships' lanterns and spread
Their illuminated costumes across their backs;

On the floors of the meadows, in the basements of the lakes,
Among the moving stairways of the air-currents and currents of
  water
In multi-level emporia it is a city made of the Big Store;

A city where the shop windows are opened wide,
Full of pubs with the alcohols circulating,
Juices of infinite electricity, and the cells of the trees
All stacked like the old smugglers' bottles, square
So they won't roll and give the game away,
Honeycombs of Irish cream and whisky; the populations
Have the freedom of the Midsummer Sales, returning home
With stouted baskets, soft goods, all the groceries of blood.

II.

The cedar-smelling water from the spring
Under the cedars; I am shopping
For black mud that is soft goods, and visit
Its night-escalator down into the lighted shop
Of the million candles under the swamp;

I am a regular customer of the wet wood and the small stream
That rounds into its velveteens and frogs; my fear
Summons the assistants who unroll the streams to let me see,
Unroll the little brook like a counter of silk,
Like the moth I enter and sip more gorgeous light-
Produce of the rock tree underground and its fruct
Of flints easing their tributory boughs slowly,
Overhead streaming with the heavenly blue juice of flints.

RAINMAKING EXERCISE

He finds the centre of the wood
Where the small switching-house or substation stands,
The circuit-breakers in their windowless brick
Creating ozonous ghost; by those transformers
He considers the golden mud digested by a spring
At the foot of an ash next to the electrical cottage,
The witchy tension streaming through the trees

For the thunder builds like an image overhead
Of its high-tension dwelling here; an ebony fort
Full of black soldiers piles its battlements,
A maze in which the lightning flickers.

Electricity and mud; the small stream
Tingles by, as the black cables wind,
As the old train sparkles by
Twangling its rails. He bares his throat

To the water and the air, for it is as if
A blind girl sees, with her throat bared.
The shadow increases, piles upon the head
As the green leaves and the red leaves
Fit together on the stream's surface
And relent into their rich brown, soft gold
For magical naughtiness in the little copse,
The mudlark among the prickle of electricity
And water, the champagne exhaled by trees
In the half-darkness just before the rain falls,
Disclosing its power. He will blacken
The white shirt to transfer its radiance inward,
Bring the black girl tumbling down
From her battlements, the inward shadow
Out into the open, and roll in it
To achieve the skin electrical, run crooked
Dodging behind the boles, a shaggy wildman
With his charged-up shadow bounding before him
Like a radar of excitement bursting with zyme.

Lightning zig-zags through the maze, immense shadows,
Immense lightnings shift among the heaped-up water,
The heavenly cities with their gunpowder disposition;
The thunderstorm is putrefaction's speediest mode;
A blacker cloud drives in, the black girl flies down
With brilliant sockets full of tears,
'I come to seek for mine eyes,' declares the rain
Opening them in every bush
And spider-web and weave of his clothing,
The heavy earthenwear with open throat;
He sees eyes opening everywhere,
Looks down and is himself eye-woven
And divines of how many sights and vestiges,
Objects, images and shades
And enigmas magic is composed, as the upper image
Falls upon the lower, and rolls in it
(This moment ebony, scented with electricity)
And takes the blind girl
By her night hand, which sees,

Who is black, because her eyes were closed,
Who has eyes when I touch her, where
I touch her, who knows
What she wishes to, with a tingle
As the current passes
Into the water, makes its union there.
The sopping clouds lean over us
For we bear in our depths
A reverse charge, which completes them, the fire
Passing into the water from the bend of the cloud
Where the serpent-lightning sneaks,
Which is the twist of the maze
Into the blind end; she
Conceals her blue flame there, zig-zagger;

The poets of water and earth
Inhale the golden air
Of their black laboratory
In the newly-built Electric City
Of dew and mud and high-tension musk:
(For the creation gave
Another smell unto me than before
Beyond what words can utter,

As in the woodly bowers,
The arbours where it rains;
And the woods suddenly
Are full of reflections,
Many evidence of worlds
Within worlds,
And herbs of consolation
Beyond expectation).

MUDLARK VI

Lily of the Valley gives gold clothes in winter,
And Apple will give deep gold,
Sloe dyes red-brown, and Iris Root
Yields a black robe. Ash offers
Gold vesture too,
And Plum blue-black garments. We are
The travelling pollinators, and we move
Into the fields like blown colours
Of the fields. Our charge for the service
Of our hives is twelve guineas a day
We roll them into Kent and set them down
To pollinate your cherries and your apples,
Into the Midlands for the flowering
Of the bean fields. When the sunlight slips
Into a glade in an especial way, declaring,
Let us say, the deep gold of Apple,
We are attentive as befits our garments
And our trade, and our word for this
Is that the equilibria are settling
With their double wings who prefer
Us dressing in these ancient root
And flower colours, following the trade
Of husbandmen and pollinators. Our young folk
Before they enter the craft, wear white; then one day
Their skins fill with invisible colours,
They yearn for all knowledge and run wild
Rolling in the yeasty marsh to learn the stains
Of all the plants at once, clothed in the tension
Of the unwritten white, and thus
The equilibria may bless them, for they emerge
Like kin of them, dyed in leaf,
And we follow them with skips
Of water, and golden
Ash-dyed shirts over our arms
To settle peace on them.

THE GOGING STOOL

The HWCH or Witch. The scribe, the scraper,
The spirit-sculptor of the Mother-of-All,
Mother of Source, the Widow, the One Alone,
Communicator. All that belonged to that firstness
Was afterwards derided and denounced but is.
Bring that to the Goging Stool, the Quagmire
Is the Accuser, choke the criminal in it,
The whore or the coward in it, the abominable
Rat of the sun in it. I will seize you
Utters every thread of this earthenwear
Until you discover in me
Your name and the name of every part of you
Which is my name.

So he is mud, walking.
He is the great decay of himself, but walking.
The green threads run into his back.
He is learned in the dumbschool.
He was recovered
On the balance-beam of the cucking-stool.
He is a lump of earth, the sod.
We might wind it in funeral flowers,
Sew in it a suit of flowers, walking,
We might plant him with wreaths,
We might bathe it white in spattering falls
And return him raining to his family
Created anew.
That lump was his dead shadow, gone on the stream.

Thus we created HWCH
In the shadows of the creek, and he was one.
He was purified in yesty ground
Bubbling with salt waters.
He was an unformed child, in his ferment.
He is close to the shadows, by our action,
If he wasn't HWCH then he is now,
Joined to his source.
We accosted him and punished him,
Assaulted him, fitted him to sin,
Member of both worlds, gatekeeper,
A route and door
And belonging to the Gog who quakes,
The bubbling, the pulsing place, the Makemire.

FLY BUDDHA

I.

Tasting the peach with the fingers,
The nap of velvet, the glittering flesh,
Recording of the Florida sun. An antelope:
Smells an orange with the slit
Under its eye. And the sensitivity of the eye

That brushes everything it sees
Several times a minute; and that
Of the painter's brush: let's look
At this painting of a talk
In a boat at night, with fireflies;
They are discussing something
Very important below the surface of life,
Every brushstroke shows it.

II.

I said to the fly, 'Get off my plate,
Go and dung-roll!' 'Sir,'
She replies irritably, as one
Who knows herself well, 'I go not to wallow,
But to feast! on incomparable suets,
And matchless custards in my finery
Of stripes and veined sunshades; and, no
You cannot say "decay": I know forest-glades
Of buttered asparagus, tree-trunks
That are whole truffle, blancmange pastures, of Cockaigne.'

III.

'Meat slides through meat,' says the fly,
'Conceive how holy to me you shit,
Like stacked Madonnas heaped with unction-flow
And rejoicing with our ancient Hum of prayer,
Our nursery-church strung with votive pearl,
Hymning. There I taste
With my whole soul,' says she,
'Which is my body, I smell with my eyes;
Odour is scenery, scenery is smell;
I scan the green grass which has travelled
Again and again through meadows
In continuous present,' 'But,' say I,
'You can speak, and reason; by that
You stand away from your joys; how can
You give yourself utterly?' 'Eigh?' asks the fly,
'What was I saying then? Please remind me.'

ADVANCED MUDLARK

Meditating in a group
In the British Iseum, a magnetic sleep
Wafts among the statues. One Isis

Condescends to wear a beautiful chalk-blue pair
Of seableached jeans.
Outside, the bird-cries

Stand still and are a ladder, and
Considering the dog's doke, his riddling
With the nose, is part of the course,

As is the mudlark in best clothes, still,
A ladder descending to the dark source
Of rainbows broken out of the black

Greasy water, universal condenser.
For all its slime it is electrical,
And each grain is a gracious glassy idol;

It is the mudlark alchemistical that harvests
Its sequent metals of the seasonal wood,
And dresses in them, that crazy source

Of spring flares and autumn asphalts
In their season, worn
On the chalkblue skyjeans, all at once. The dog

Tucked underneath her arm comes to the mudlark;
He watches with his nose his mistress
Entering absolutely everything, her trouser-firmament

Completely blotted. This Mistress,
Says the Dog, has forgotten;
For her the world has grown opaque

So she needs this black-metal mirror
To pass through and the lean
Silver streams sewing

Ample morass, and to drabble
Her perfection with this completeness; she needs my nose,
For to me the world transforms

(As she knows well) with every faceting
Change of the wind anywhere,
As in this wood paved with deep glasses of its alloys,

So I can see the woodland metals she is gathering
Stoned with her changes, like robes about her
Or a Stone of perfume, and her soiled face rises

Magicked with the relenting source
Above its bath and calls to me
Knowing her Dog again: 'My Eft,' she cries, 'my purpose,

My Imp, my Imperial Imp, my Work, my Worry, my purpose.

MUDLARK X

As in ‘those thin-filled Mappes we yet
Finde the name of Walsingham’ I am lying in mud
From whence the winds are generated
Looking for the small town
That lies behind everything.

I smell this town with noble avenues, but as yet
See only mud upon my body. I rise
And brush it off my clothes
Though it leaves
Great Mappes and cold breath.

I can smell that other Town
With the ancient ebony lanes,
The slate phosphorescent with the rain,
In the winged hives among the strawberry canes,
Such disparates, in the white castle
That is the clay refinery, in the cargo-vessel
White with the mud of china clay,
Solid white even in its black holds;

The small town is its other cargo,
The small town behind this small town that I smell
And hear now in the bee-hum, the engine-thud, the black mud’s
Grunt as I turn round in it.

My wife played lute to me as I washed the longe Mappes off,
My charts of navigation to the Smalle Towne,
And as she played her instrument to me
That bathroom gave admittance to the Smalle Towne
And I could fling the smalle windowe open and call nakede
To my bathfellows, and when I did this
The sun that belonged to Walsingham
Shone on these docks as well. I donned
An ordinary shirt and trousers, fitting garb
That recalls a dreamer's clothes, or pyjamas,
Unisex, and while we ate I saw
At our table twenty priests and priestesses
Dining post-coitally in candlelight
From Walsingham. I knew
It was where the man with cold breath lived,
But when you drew nearer to his house of Mudde
His breath grew warme, smelling of seaweed,
And visible, like Mappes of noble tides.

MUDLARK
(For Sylvia)

I.

Rolling in the mud
Will bring her back,
Will bring the sun back,
Will bring the summer on,
The human skin
Bristled as by the electricity
Of the growing land;
Rolling in the mud,
Gathering the zyme.
She sighed
Once or twice,
Then shuddered, then died,
The sigh of a meditation,
The complete relaxation.
In the ploughed field roll,
Between the wet furrows
The mortal panting.
Death is so terrible
God alone should bring it.
My organs have gone cold
With her death,
The cups of meat
Which were eyes.
Under the sun the warm mud
Greens its face,
Unlids its flowers.

II.

Rolling in the socket,
In the dead eye,
The bird balancing the evening,
Turning its mortices,
The fly unlidding its wings;
In the clay is hidden
A white dove,
And a mineral sun
Is set in this firmament.
I hear my mortal panting
Like a bed-partner's breathing,
The head in the belly nods
Once or twice, and sighs;
It is a little death.
I repair to the laboratory,
The bedroom within the rock,
The sweet fruct of scoriae,
I am clothed in rust
The hue of silver-tarnish,
Look for me, I am an unseen
With my low cave of forme,
My imprint, and I pass unseen;
I am one of her kind now;
The mud relents
And a sigh from its depths
Unlids my skin, again.

GRAND BUVEUR

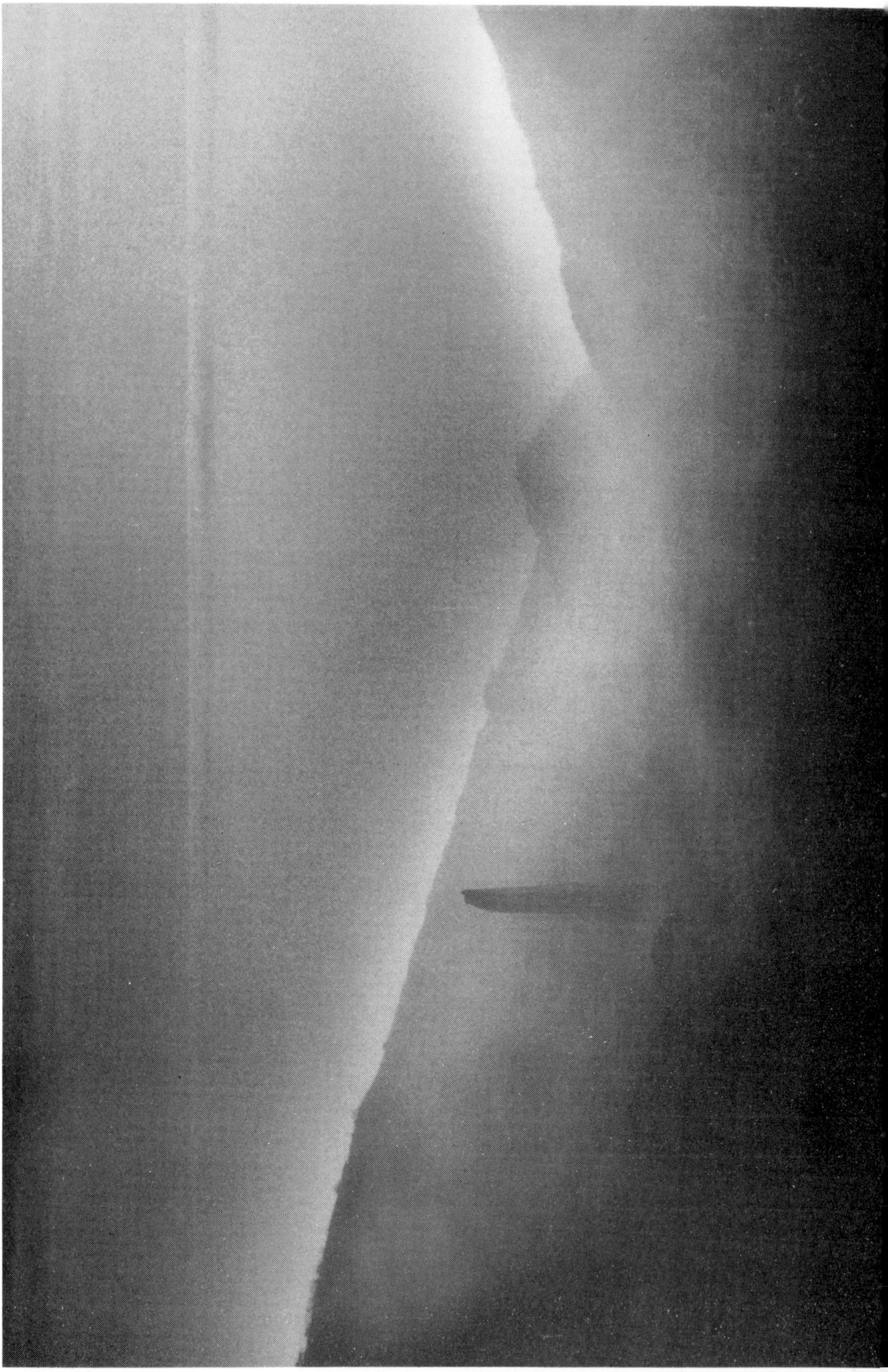

DRINK TO THE DUKE

The Duke of Burgundy, who represents
The drunkenness of battle,
With the deep purple of its soldiers,
Those bottles of hot blood
Caved in immense tuns
Under the battle-field, bottlefield,
Where it travels with its iron into the grapes;
Burgundy, you are drinking soldiers,
And have always done so—

And the Duke in his iron rage,
His moustache erect, his eyes bolting,
Reining his horse so she stands
Huge on her hind legs,
And the great insect carapace leaning sideways
With its white eyes in the coal-scuttle helmet
Glaring like the soul of a mantis,
And the noble sword scything down,
Uncorking you, drinking you by the neck.

GRAND BUVEUR I

Two barmaids play by squirting beer,
Soak each other from the taps; a miniature
Of champagne shaken by a bar-squire,
With his finger as a nozzle, leaps in spray so
The room floats with zest and spiritous dew
Like the holy Celonese festival of white-shirted girls
Squired by squirted coloured waters
So that soon everybody is rainbows after a ritual storm.

Drunkenness arrives
As in the darkroom
Fluttering in alchemical trays
The vision on red paper in black silver is suddenly complete;

Or as the dew
Forming with perfect bell-roundness
Like bells of glass in harmony
Rings echoes of itself on every grass-blade,
Harmony of lenses, each reflecting all,
Dew suddenly there like knowledge,
Over the surfaces of the brain the perfect nerve-dew
Arriving in the grey meadows of brain,
Like drunkenness, complete.

And the depth of his drinking suddenly fits
End to end like all the pints fastened
Into a glass-lined well that reaches through the years
He calls down it and echoes call him back
To a Sunday walk on a Somerset hill by an orchard
Where the boy lay down having bought cider
From Farmer Gregory, virgin cider
Harvested by virgins, purchased by them, and dreamed
A fabled animal pacing through the trees,
A deer with silver antlers between which spun the moon,
Pacing through the big dew of apples formed to perfection,
Every bristle of its pelt sharp, but within
The black dews steady in the violin velvet skull
His image trapped.

PICK-ME-UP

A dream inspired by reality,
In his seat by the window
Of the pub which is the throne and palace of so many;
A dream inspired by swallowing,
By swallowing and breathing a special air
Made of grey, and tumbling.
The Brides of Cornwall in their rough-hewn temples,
Their rude granite rooflessness,
Stone pillars, moonbeam rafters,
And the mothy doors of long grasses,
The ceiling of fire-flecked soot which is the sky,
And stars on her breath
Of such a one, initiate's starry breath, the gulls
Swarm over the fishing-boat returning
With their oily catch, fluttering
Like stars on her breath . . .

Thus a Fall Graduate of Whisky
Visiting Falmouth for a tavern pick-up, the pigeons
Dab-dabbing around with their big leaning breasts
Like old ship figureheads. She fills
The pewter mug, the soft foam rises
Pouting like the breast of a dove,
The bubbles cooing a round astonished sound,
Turning crisp pounds to sparkling urine.
Intoxicated by the ceiling of stars,
The violin-brown concert of beer,
Lungs kippered dry with smokes,
Coughing like a choppy sea,
Crisp-pissing out the pound notes,
The white chrysalids of tobacco
Passing through the fire to unwrap themselves,
He ascends on dove-grey pinions
To the sea-breezes out of the carrion window.

MASTER PISS-ON-HIMSELF
(Universal Pissoir)

It is the garden
Of Master Piss-on-Himself
Who made the dew.

He causes the trumpets to roar
As he indicates the falls
Abounding in their multitudes.

His votives are the grassy shrines of tiles
In continuous baptism and imageless union
With the dew. He caused the lashing tempest.
He rounded the fat drops of the unctuous shower.

The wet turns all our rags to silk.
The rain rings lightly on the rims
As the squall drives through the belfries.
It is the park of Master Piss-on-Himself,
His groves are big grass whose mossy trunks
Glitter with peppery springs all night, all day.

THE SHINING

I notice what shines, now. Look!
The Moon is the night-snake
That shakes and walks in the long water;

Look, returning in the sunlight,
Dragonflies still as chipped obsidian;
Returning through the wheatfield,

The Sabbath husking of the corn, the heart torn
And eaten out of its summery tabernacle.
And thus telesma issues from the celebrants,
The shining metal that plates the walls

With gold, only I cannot say
It is precisely gold.

The golden fountain caught in the priestly robe
Tied at the neck with a white band
Pouring from underneath his petticoats
So that he plashes as he walks
A breakfast of elixirs.

APRÈS-BOIRE

A button on his blue shirt disturbs my sleep
Like a wheel, a wheeled cross with its thread,
Horloge of the occasions I have breathed

An electrical flash in the blessed perfume of his chest.
His bamboo stick is the best symbol of the gentleman
Due to its upright bearing and its inner humbleness,

A hollow sunbeam, its inner emptiness, the gentleman
Who is intellectual yet mindless, and I
Am the lady of the bruised pillow of his nights.

Let him have a few-and-a-half beers and consider
With his uprightness whether the frill of her dress
Is an opening or an erection;

The electrical flash passes between their breasts,
The great wheel spins down into the chest,
The round rainbow rolling of the liquid lightning,
The self-revolving wheel of opening and closing
Time.

ALCHEMICAL BUVEUR

The chemicals, the pure liqueurs, the world's metals,
The rows of bottles charged in their heirarchy,
The seven human metals, distilling in the breath,
The slow coppered snake of beer
Winding among fundamentals,
Leaping forth
Into its nest of urine, its foaming nest.

How but with close pellets of kiss and pulse
Shall we build our castle of the heart?
The lips thus part, and the legs thus speak.

Yet once again the close castle falls; the persuasive juke-box
Feels its way between those pulses,
Prizes the stones apart,
And the clear metal of gin
Winds its way through the foundations; again at the swinging doors

A sudden cool draught says they are back.

M. GRENADINE

Tipping his topper
Just off his pale brow to show the sweatband,
A poster of le patron
To publicise the restaurant,
Offering a peach in his outstretched hand denoting
Long life, and to the yonis, devotion.
The restaurant in the bookshop, with listening-booths,
And the shore on which it stands a kind of bookshop
As cleanly-paged and juiced as his fresh melons,
All the waves marvellous non-fiction,
And the bookshop the longest of the shore-shells,
Coiling into its booths,
Alive with interesting echoes.
What is a poet, then?
Quips the patron, grinning like a serpent,
Pointing to his tree-shaded restaurant.
Why, every summer in my melon-beds
Snakes lay down broad chains of dimpled eggs
In a world that is without shadow to them,
For everything flowing ripples,
And all flows, and is as mystic
As the orchestras from the turntables.
It is the resting-state of animals,
The peristaltic vision after dining,
Remarks the patron from every poster
Standing with his top hat uplifted and peach cleft
In its ghostly fuzz or nap,
Advertising his restaurant-record-cum-bookshop,
Its harmonising salons of alcohol and sugar
And lights of juice in costly velveteen
Orchestral darkness, and with long life
In the uplifting alcohol of yonis, toasted.

LEGIBLE HOURS

The legibility of the evening,
The union of grapes,
We drink it and its spiritous consummation
In this brandy that shines in the dark within,
With the lamps blowing,
The flames like enraged tigers
Roaring in their thin glittering cages,
Ravenous oil-eaters.

The stinking shadows fly out of the wooden windows.
In the dawn, the brittle machine of salt,
The salt bread of the sea, fish for breakfast,
Feathery skeleton, pinion of the sea;
On the smooth-spun sand
Imprint of constellations,
Starcast of the brine, starfish.

Then the evening made legible
By the recording of a ghost
Or an opera of ghosts, the impress,
The mediumistic conches attending, the ear-shells,
The ghost's whorls spinning in their skirts,
Her contractions and ululations,
Her abyssing to her still axle,
Her repeats, her expansion
To the night sky, circling,
The display and occultation
On the night air of her grave that turns.

The legibility of the house.
The courtyard tree,
Green harbour of ten thousand ships
Tending anchor, optical toy of deep shade;
Can you hear the light hum circling in echoes
Around the stream, and the reflections
Caught in the woods and the inextricable shadows
All combing one way, can you? and there!
As the tide turns the weir-sound changes
Its pictures and the tree-head lightens
In the legibility of the grape and the new morning.

GRAND BUVEUR XI
(Emergency Ward)

A clean young doctor hurtles past
With his bag, carrying with him an exhalation,
A bouquet of medical alcohol,
Medical clean sweetness,

And when he enters the white building
Dons a coat as white as alcohol and its walls,
A roomy white through which the vapours roll
And distil from patients' lungs on gurney metal
Where an ambulance siren scribbles the air,

The river of car-roofs fondling the sun
The disc that appears and disappears in them
The siren screams at them;

At home, the baby, her little fingers
Scrabbling at the bedstead as if afraid of falling

There is a paediatric flow
Of medically-scented air through the nursery
Striking with its clean sword
At the delicate mayblossom odour
Of the baby's skin

Outside the window
I see a bird sitting in an odorous limetree,
It opens its beak and utters thunder;

I toss back my layman's gin, my doctor;
It strikes like lightning.

TO THE HABITUÉS

I.

The pub is the Tap, Taproot, Tolgate
To behind-the-appearance-of-things
Where what is decayed becomes not only interesting
But intoxicating too, spirit and inspiration,
Holding my breath while drinking, on my journey
To the brilliant underworld of four-fold cider
Lighted with a million daily glasses in candlelight.

II.

My insulation is leaky, and the cider seals
Me with a colourful apple-skin. And too

III.

Environmental, for I feel the changes
And the flows and need to contain
These fluxes in my cider-glass, brimming
With apple-round liquor, small circuit.

IV.

When the central heating comes on
With its clang in all rooms, it is like
A blow on the bars of a cage by a great
Water-paw, and the animals
Of water chase each other round the Point
And balance for an instant, as the tides
Change, he-tide on she's back, still for an instant.

V.

And the clouds, the air-fronts cresting,
Heavy waves that grind your neck down
To pray your nose into your glass, and the spirits
And the barometers drop, the glass is falling,
So the same again, please.

VI.

The whirl between the two waters of the Point
Like eyeballs flickering about to sleep,
About to wake, why don't they drop off,
Sketching their energies in white
Tinted with amber glasses.

VII.

The seeing face-to-face, over a glass, the world
No longer continuously perceived but continually drunk up,
And recreated; the forms of the eternal world
Are those constantly perceived in this one
At still instants of the flicker
Of glasses across the bar, recurring rite
That stops the world, for a moment;
They should make them deeper, these
Amber instants, flickering,

VIII.

As we enter and leave as through swinging doors
Through the lid or mirror of the wine and cider,

Which has a few dead apple-blossoms floating on it.

NEXT TO THE RESERVOIR

To feel the correction to the atmosphere
Like the near presence of a waterfall in nature
As the bubbling brook that walked here gushes

From the penis next to me in the stalls,
A rising pitch as the trough fills,
I steal a glance at him; a mouth

That seems to find in its own
Deep depravity a cause for amusement;
Hale fellow, well hung. The beer

Causes you to feel well and whole,
Borrowing a little health from the future.
Back through the little garden,

The mould-marbled apples still clinging
To the dwarfish tree. At the bar
She presses her pretty loinbones

Against me like the slender pillars
Of a marble palace. Sometimes the band
Plays degenerate guitars and sometimes

Hollow banjos, an instrument which cannot
Be played slowly. Tonight
There is an atmosphere of guitars

And a perspective of watery voices
Discussing the next day's races over the reservoirs.

GRAND BUVEUR IX

The lungs like two dogs intertwined
Biting each other to the same heart,
Catarrh expelled with a bark

Like a potent semen, a virile custard.
A pint, another amber portal
Every ten minutes for four hours only.

The shivering Will-O'-the-Wisp-
Aspen-cut matches. Glass
Threshold after threshold,

Stained-glass doorways that lift up,
Float down. The brown marshes
Of tobacco flickering

With those same delusive flames that graze
The brown moss rhythmically,
That tremble in the trembling hand.

Glass-sucker and piss-artist,
Beer-press and whittler of ale
Off its stout tuns, slimming them,

Making them his own measure
Which leaks and increases.
He has too the wings of smoke

The fat-bodied pints flying away
On the grey plumage unfurling.
In order to enter these precincts

And stay there, one must
As far as possible be changed
Into a mad dog or a stout devoted water-drop.

GRAND BUVEUR X

To endeavour by drinking to condense
As far as possible the all-pervading
Mother-body of water, to become

One of her whole and rounded bald glisters.
As the web drinks the dew
And displays its coruscations

So the body brims
With burning internalised
Self-interest, like light in drops.

The mind becoming water skims
With transient patterns like the waterflies.
I stroke her web, says the fly,

Which is pearled with icons,
I stroke her glittering moisture,
I stroke her silk,

I am captivated
Says the falling-down
Glass-reversing brittle acrobat

Of the lipped trapezes that tilt
On slow ropes that have elbows.

WINE LAKE

The waves spread out
To the arch of heaven
Waiting to deal their blow,
My Tv
On its peninsular kicking into the sea;
I adjust the positions
Of its walls of reverberations
To a programme of wine-tasting;

Figures appear in the glass, for now
The coloured pictures are stacked to the heights
And small taps open great altitudes

As the wine undresses in its glass,
Its sudden bouquet of person,
Its fleurie,

Between the white-clad tables
Its individual note
That is its flowers of self.

The demonic is the sudden
Just as a spider streaks in any of
Eight sudden directions, plucking
The ceiling from its white contemplation
To apprehension of its stains and cracks,
Its attics thundering to the small rain;

And in the chapel of the monastery of stone
Whose dimensions have been tuned for centuries
The sudden may streak out like that spider
In wine like black lightning.
So much air has been shaped there
And perfume formed by throats
That sipped the fruct, and it is tuned
By all the psalms
To the fragrance of Emmaus;
Its candle-grease is ashes of that light
Which dances through my television set
Clothed in my wine.

For when the Son is married to his Bride
The Father becomes sweeter than human,
Teaching his children to couple,
Bending over the married pair on the bed,
Adjusting them to each other,
The whole chamber
Tuned to hypnotism and flickering with ichor,
And the sweet bouquet of the siblings,

And a certain sixty-foot burden of the trees
Outside the open churchdoor,
Trees of the churchyard
Recording so many years' reverbatory growth;
And, alas, our wine-polluted lungs
Like the travel-stained sails of tall ships
Warping it may be into harbour
Steered by the flicker of the bloody tower.

GRAND BUVEUR VIII

The sealed book of his heart
Full of scrolls of oxygen
Bursts its lockets
And the locket at his neck bursts
The tall vein there ripped off like a tie
His collar exploding,
The grenade of his heart,
And in the sudden heat and light
The lungs open wide their gates
With a great shout *Zohar*!

His whole vocabulary
All the words he has spoken, whispered, sung,
In one shout
That is stout
Like a dictionary snatched
Out of the fire and flung
Over the abyss flaming,
A star shattering into words of every hue;

The electrical bine
Piped in vertebral thorns
Shook and slowly reddened,
St. Elmo's fire at every fingerprint,
A corona of slow-motion burning
Like a Christmas pudding of illuminated brandy
Carried in in its holly crown
With its sweet smell of blood and fruit
Full of silver money
Slack bag of money and pudding slowly
Slumping to the spittle floor
Among the tobacco embers
The teeth gnawing aslant in the head
Like a pudding eating itself

And the too-many birds of his soul
In the threshing of his blood tree
The birds which should be one bird
Beating its wings steadily in his heart
Fluttered everywhere
Catching St. Elmo's fire
And flew with greater wings of flame
In oiled colours up his chimney
And the carrions of him sparkled like soot upflying
Buzzing sparks of the hearth

All the spirits flew up and sideways

And the soul fell back
And dove into sappy rock
Rejoining the water it was made of
And lay in strata
Like wardrobes
Like crisp shirts
Slowly purified in the laundries of geology and pressed
Slowly slowly into new ghost
Rising in vents fumaroles and drains
Just a hint of him here
To his friends in that gutter
In the babbling of that gutter-voice
Or returning from its carousals in the sky
Like rain, and not like a ghost

And in cold winter
Lying like crisp shirts ready to be worn again
Surprised and finding themselves
So clean and sparkling with such cool colours
And folded in such silence after that fat brief bloody shout.

DRUNK, BUT NOT TOO DRUNK

Grain is slaughtered by pounding it
Musically to obtain its spirit, which
Will show you everything; the spirits in music
Are audible to the point of visibility. Death?
Why, the skyshell chiming like this rubbed glass
To the blows of the militant chick-beak and
The jagged sky falls away
From the starfeathered bosoms beyond.

There are sighted dreams and musical dreams
And who shall say which is the wiser?
The baby slides out like a quiet at sea
And a mark on the water like the hull of a ghost-ship;
The silences of tattered webs hang in the hedge
Like torn letters of the alphabet
And silken scores for golden flies; the music
Sliding from trombones like bewitched butter
Peers into the eyes of all the people
Caught in the blind dream. Butter:
How amazing that is!
Bewitched mud!
By all the grass-roots and the cows bewitched.

MAGIC

I.

Something passed between their eyes,
An imprint passes,
A rearrangement fused with a recognition;
Then she dreamed
That the evil but fascinating man was in prison
But he sailed out of that in a huge ship with masts of gold
Full of black people sacrificing,
And he on the poop
Where his silver staff or stick of captainship
Does not mimic but is the moon's full beam.

II.

So I find that I
Have prepared myself by weeks of abstinence
For a descent into alcoholic flux
As life is turned into a dream and a black sacrifice
By galleons of Guinness and the grey
Ectoplasmic corpses of burnt cigarettes,
Their bodies swelling to invisibility,
And then in a pub something passes between eyes,
A melting followed by a rearrangement,
Followed by a forgetting, alas.

And that day I left my silver toothpick
Somewhere in the bar, I believed it would
Have to be forgotten,
But it is returned to me by one
Who disdains to take advantage of a drunk man,
And as she hands the smoky silver staff to me
A recognition passes and I wish it were hers.

LOCAL
(For G.M.)

The Quiet Woman; the pub where men sat suckling
In the silence; a joke against wives. She was headless
Yet her benefits flowed; she was tongueless
Because we would not listen to her. A joke
Against drinkers. The Son it was
Who listened, whom the womb magnified from His dot,
Who entered shining with it, and returned, the Word
Arising always from the liquid mind, again,
There, as you see it, again there,
The Ever-Coming One, the same
Again, please.

The Ash outside the local is the tree of life
Because it hisses in the wind like serpents;
The midwife takes a stick of green ash
And thrusting one end into the fire
As it burns, receives the sap from the raw end into a spoon,
And gives it to the child for its first tipple;
That was a fortunate child who then could see
And remember with more than the five senses
Of Aristotle; and the lochial ash dropping
Its little veined keys into the warp of water.

His bedlinen upon rising smells of cucumber
And nothing more. Orion stands at ease,
Unbuckled, just above the horizon,
All the moored yachts swaying slightly,
Rattling their bolts and tackle on a tide
That tastes pleasantly, with a savour of cucumber;
Was this how a Saviour might taste?
In this light breeze that smells of cucumber,
The thousand trees that moan because they could be made
Into a hundred thousand yachts or violins.

This is his milestone, by the ash. The Moon
Sinks into it every midsummer. I lust
To sleep, and dream; out of the windows
I watch the misty dunes that are moored
And suddenly on a cold wind their low cloud clears
And their sands pour with its distillates,
The cool dunes, the immense quartz distillaries
Like a multifarious waterworks condense the dew,
Foaming suddenly with dew-brooks and freshets,
A gigantic fractionation. How can
Such beauties be tongueless! Listen,
The great dew condenses in the Quiet Woman's belly,
The unborn child, the secret sharer of the bed,
The inward drinker of The Quiet Mother,
The child who when he is crowned will light the whole city.

BUVEUR AT POETRY READING

The red stars that live on but fade
In the brown mother of tobacco;
The amber mother of beer;

A brown room seen through a glass
With the gardens of tobacco and beer flowering,

And paper lily-flowers with their
Red-tipped brown pistil and their
Pollen of cancer, the cigarette-flowers
Greying the human lung-parks,

Mouldy, broken branches in the breath-wind.
The trumpeting, brass-flavoured quid.

I speak aloud the great psalms in order to breathe
And lay everywhere the small quivering eggs of spit,

The great night-flyer of my lungs.

This mother, she has no eyes,
But the amber blind do not see that,
They have autumn sockets, full of the fruct,

She rents us certain eyes to see.

The wide dove wings of tobacco,
The great brown bosom of the warm beer,

The partners glide upstairs
Into the Hall of Drinking Clothes;

The natural electricity
Of her fawn trousersuit

Declares her energy,
Planted with svelte wheat

Each hair of a million
Stirs visibly.

GRAND BUVEUR II

An impure
Draughty tourbillion opens in my throat
With the desire for a smoke. I resist
For a space, and only for a space, otherwise
The evening would be spoilt. The spirit of tobacco, sure,
Is a greater power than the individual cigarette,
And there is an abyss between immaculate and filthy,
Cause for rejoicing; I pollute myself carefully.

Drunk, and smoking, he sees
The qualities of things and not their consequences;
Friends, I was afraid, the swift-drawing flue
Of her white neck in the soot-hued dress
Is of such quality, and I cannot know
The consequences. The little pat
Of butter melted between her thighs,
The butter. I had the feeling of my seed
Rooting, a feeling of rotation
As of parachutes winding into groves
Of bamboo, thick-set, the summation.
She shakes the rain off the tree-pattern on her blouse,
She shines like a peacock in the wet,
In the rain, she flowers, her cigarette goes out,
As I tread in her stream
There is no space or time, my hand passes
Into her collar, a clean wet tourbillion.

ON THE DUNES
(Grand Buveur)

He dreams a white braid on the back of her head;
He nodded off. A cold presence wakes him,
Like the door of a meat-freezer
Left wide open, and a blizzard of broken glass
Showers the pub-lawns until they are sparkling and white.

A glass of beer wings its way, a sandwich
Welds him to this world.
It is the pub on the dunes, and in the wind
A silky piskie face of mothwing texture
Flutters over the rolling sand
Lost and re-emerging
Among the dots and streaks of shadow;
Does the whisky trapeze
Sustain it? Best
To mackle all day in the pub, among the televisions
And the pleasant fruit of comedy,
For, among the rocks and sands,
There are many things that poke around
And snip snip watch. The wan light descends
Of an early moon full of moths,
The moon is full of moths, fluttering,
The moon rides on wings of moth,

While the hairdresser works late in his lighted salon
On the dunes, still scissoring, shampooing, waving,
Rinsing, twisting, perming, blow-drying,
And will continue to do so past closing-time.
For whom? The night-folk. The night-hairdresser.
It is his moonlit salon, among the braids
Of dune-sand plaited high as the moon.

THE ONEIRIC EXERCISE
(Grand Buveur)

They drink a foam of domestic profit;
The sky-blue breath of the tobacco addict,
The skyclad breath of the inner skin,

Flies from the lungs, the inner parks,
Those angelic wings veined with tremendous effort;
And the pint pots that are holes in time,

Corridors of glass of a separate duration.
Play of the sea and the small rain outside;
Precious moments in the fair field.

He is performing the oneiric exercise;
Stone rivers slowed, the curtain folds
Of mental mountains; he peers

Into the amber goblet; it is dreamfull;
He glances out and thinks the hovercraft
Is a ship on fire blowing fierce

And torrential smoke out of its skirts;
And how spectral that wire-netting in the waste-ground looks
Rolled up like the skin of some snake

Down from those folded mountains
Having cast its diamond slough of nettle-venom.
My hundred pints.

I am sat here to drink them for a wager,
My hundred eyes like Argus,
Whose head was packed like the sun with them,

Thus my empty glasses and my full ones circle me,
My empty and my full eyes,
The watchful eyes and the sockets near sleep.

When I have finished
My hundred eyes will be shrouded in a single darkness;
With the Immortal, only two

Would at any time take rest, the remainder watchful.

First published in 1986
by Rivelin Grapheme Press
199 Greyhound Road London W14 9SD

Printed in England by The Devonshire Press, Torquay

British Library Cataloguing in Publication Data

Redgrove Peter
The Mudlark Poems & Grand Buveur
I. Title
821′. 914 PR 6035. E267
ISBN 0–947612 21 1

The photographs are by Carole Bruce.

Of this edition 26 copies have been lettered A to Z and signed by the Author.

Rivelin Grapheme Press
London 1986